Fannie A Damon

Heart Treasures

Fannie A Damon

Heart Treasures

ISBN/EAN: 9783744665810

Printed in Europe, USA, Canada, Australia, Japan

Cover: Foto ©Thomas Meinert / pixelio.de

More available books at **www.hansebooks.com**

HEART TREASURES

BY

FANNIE A. DAMON

AUTHOR'S EDITION

BUFFALO
CHARLES WELLS MOULTON
1894

PRINTED BY
CHARLES WELLS MOULTON,
BUFFALO, N. Y.

To the kind Sisters and Friends

in this life,

and in tender memory of the Loved Ones

gone before

I dedicate this book.

CONTENTS.

HEART TREASURES

HEART TREASURES.

WHEN we lay aside the garments
    That our loved ones used to wear;
And our tears fall thick and blindly
On each trinket, tress of hair—

On each token of remembrance
    Their dear hands have laid away—
Treasures they have prized as fondly
    As the ones we hold to-day;

When we feel that all is over,
    As the shadows round us fall,
Then we question in our anguish,
    Vainly asking, " Are these all?"

" All that's left us of our loved ones,
    These, and but a bitter pain,
And a sorrowing heart that ever
    Yearns to call them back again."

But have we not dearer tokens
    Than the ones o'er which we weep?
They will perish, but the others,
    We can ever with us keep.

They are ours through time and changes;
  Death can not these treasures claim;
For the *good*, the *true*, the *lovely*
  Ever will with us remain.

For the heart hath secret chambers
  Filled with stores of wealth untold;
Costly relics, that can never
  Like earth's gems be bought and sold.

Precious memories of our loved ones;
  Visions of a happy past,
That will never fade or vanish,
  But grow brighter to the last.

A RETROSPECT.

GONE the swift years, with ceaseless, noiseless
    flight!
  We can but gaze through Memory's glass to-
    night!
But as our eyes in sadness on them fall,
Are we not prone to question, '' Is this all?''

All that there is of life—a few brief years—
Made up of joy and sadness, smiles and tears?

Like April days, of sunshine and of rain,
A moment bright, then clouded o'er again.

Yet *more*, the past hath *more*; can we not see
Days bright with blessings rich, for you and me?
Without a cloud to dim, or hide God's light;
Perfect, unchangeable, from morn till night?

And for *these* days, our Father, would we praise,
And thank thee, who hath ordered all our ways;
But not alone by blessings are we blest,
For those withheld, ofttimes have proved the best.

For we have thus been led to trust thy ways,
Nor find our all, in joy's unclouded rays;
True happiness is not made up of years,
But blessedness is ofttimes born of tears.

And as we gaze upon the past's rich store
That still is ours, and count it o'er and o'er;
Number the blessings, in His mercy given,
And all the joys, that's made of earth a heaven;

We will no longer question in our pain
What of the past! What good doth yet remain?
But make the joys and sorrows yet to come,
As stepping-stones, to lead us farther on.

LIFE'S LESSONS.

HOW shall I gather the fragments up
　　That nothing be lost? she said;—
　Or improve the hours that are flitting past,
　Ere they make up a day that is dead?

How can I unravel the knotted skein
　With dark and with bright hues rife?
Or pick up the broken tangled threads
　That I've wove in this web of life?

How make the disjointed useless parts
　Of earth's broken idols complete?
Or find the lost chord in Life's Melody grand,
　That made such harmony sweet?

How bear the burdens of sorrow and care
　That are on my shoulders laid,
With cheerful and uncomplaining heart
　And a soul, that is undismayed?

———

By making the trials of every day
　Yield a harvest of peace and love;
By counting the blessings of every hour,
　As thy kindly descend from above.

By carefully watching the bright design,
    The pattern God gives me to weave—
With patience striving to mend the threads
    Of error, o'er which I now grieve.

By toiling on with a fearless heart,
    Though my burden heavier grows;
It will lighter be, and scarcely felt,
    If I lighten another's woes.

If I dry the tear on the mourner's cheek,
    With the comfort that God in His love
Will make earth's broken idols complete
    In his mansions in Heaven above.

IN MEMORIAM.

SPEAK but thy name, how swift the tide
    Of feeling overflows;
  But while we question vainly, oft,
  'Tis only God who knows—

Knows why thy promising young life
    So early was cut down,
Or why thy earthly cross was changed
    Into a heavenly crown.

The cross thou bore so bravely, well,
　　Through sickness and through pain,
Now laid aside, the conflict o'er,
　　The heavenly conquest gained.

"Thank God I've won!" O brave young soul!
　　Though short thy earthly life
O'er death thou'st gained the victory
　　O'er worldly pain the strife.

No more will earthly doubts perplex
　　Thy sensitive young heart,
For now thou knowest all the joys
　　That late thou knew but part.

How sweet, how glad, thy welcome home!
　　How trustingly thou laidst
Thy hand in his all-loving one
　　When powerless we to aid.

And though our hearts are sore with grief,
　　Thy voice above we hear
In sweet familiar words that breathe
　　Comfort and hope and cheer,

Saying, "Dear ones, no longer grieve,
　　I'm with you as of old,
To cheer, to comfort and to bless
　　With heavenly love untold.

"Look up and smile; the cloud that fills
 With earthly grief the space
Twixt you and me, shall lifted be,
 And you'll behold my face."

THE AWAKENING.

WHY talk of Death at Easter-time
    When all about us speaks of Life?
  When Nature's throbbing, pulsing heart,
With powers of darkness is at strife.

When the long night of rest is o'er,
 And Earth awakened from her sleep,
Thrills with new light and warmth and power,
 As through her veins the life-blood creeps.

A tinge of life is on the woods;
 A breath of life floats on the air;
A hint of life the brown earth gives,
 Of verdure, bloom, beyond compare.

Then talk no more of pain and death,
 Or aught that fills the soul with gloom;
Weep not, O sorrowing child of earth,
 Above the dark and moulding tomb!

For Death is but the Gate of Life!
    The birth, whereby the soul attains
To greater heights, diviner love,
    Than earth bound mortals e'er could gain.

And only we, who, blind to sight,
    See not the light, feel not the power,
Renounce the all-embracing Love,
    That still sustains us hour by hour.

O may we wake from this dull sleep,
    To conquer Death, to end the strife!
Renew our inward powers and feel
    How blest a thing is Life, true Life!

TO-DAY.

TO-DAY my soul! take heed to-day!
    Fast flies Time's shuttle; soon the web,
    The warp and woof of human life,
    Will all be woven, thread by thread!
To-morrow is not yet begun;—
    Darkness and silence lies between!
We can not lift the veil that hides
    The future, though we sit and dream,

Or backward call the yesterdays—
    The past, whose dead and withered flowers
Lie strewn along the path we tread;
    Reminders of life's wasted hours!

O doubting soul, no more delay
    Nor longer wait to-morrow's dawn!
For lo! the shadows flee away,
    The mists arise, and bright the morn,
The herald of another day
    Is dawning on the darkened sight!
Then waste it not in idle fears,
    But strive and labor, ere the night
Find thee with listless folded hands,
    Dreaming, with all life's work undone;
Counting with pain the yesterdays,
    Waiting the morrows, that will never come!

CHRISTMAS MEMORIES.

CHRISTMAS anthems now are swelling,
    Christmas carols fill the air;
And the music of their ringing,
    Echoing on the frosty air,
Fills my soul with tenderest longing,
    Longing for the days now fled,
Ere my eyes knew aught of weeping
    Or my heart mourned for its dead.

How sweet memories come thronging
    As upon the past I gaze,
As I hear the Christmas chimings
    Of the bells of other days;
When my heart was light and happy,
    As we gathered round the hearth,
When the circle was unbroken,
    Where was Christmas joy and mirth.

Now the merry Christmas greeting
    Has no music in its tone;
And the Christmas' sun it shines not
    With the warmth that then it shone;

For my life is in a shadow,
  And my ears are deaf to sound,
So I can not hear the music
  Of the angel choirs around,

As they shout the glad Hosannas;
  I can only catch the strain,
Echo of the long lost voices
  I have listened for in vain.
But a peace that passeth knowledge,
  Comes my saddened heart to cheer,
As I seem to hear them speaking
  As of old, in tones most dear,

Saying, " Dear one cease your grieving!
  Do not think of us as gone,
For we'll come again unto you,
  And our stay will not be long;
We are ever yours in spirit,
  O, be glad this Christmas tide!
For though absent, we are present,
  And though dead, have *never* died."

PRAYER FOR THE DEAD.

WE pray for near and distant friends;
  Ah! why not for the *dead* as well?
Are they so far removed, they need
No thought or word of ours, to tell

The longing of our inmost souls?
  The love their absence but inspires?
The thoughts that shape themselves in words,
  Wishes and hopes and fond desires

Breathed in the Father's listening ear?
  That He will keep within His care
The dear departed ones as well
  As those for whom our nightly prayers

Are offered at His throne of grace:—
  For *all* are sharers of His love;
Whether as dwellers on the earth,
  Or as the sainted dead above.

For have they still no thought of us?
  Then why should not our spirits blend
In sweet communion, and our prayers
  Alike for each, to God ascend?

Why need they not our prayers, our love?
  For what *is* prayer, but love expressed?
Fond hopes and wishes; more than these;
  Our deepest wants to God confessed!

And will He not from out His love
  Grant us the boon our sad hearts crave?
Are not the loved and early lost
  Still, still our own beyond the grave?

For death can not divide our souls;
  'Tis only sin can keep from us
The love these yearning spirits feel
  For us, weak children of the dust.

And shall the love their prayers evoke
  Find no response within our heart?
O, let us bear the idols hence
  That keep us from their souls apart!

And let our prayers in their behalf,
  (Feeble petitions, though they be),
Be echoed from their blest abode,
  And find response, O Lord, with Thee!

LINES ACCOMPANYING A PICTURE.

IT is only the *shadow* you see dear,
　When you gaze on this pictured face,
Which may grow dim with the dust of years,
And lose its freshness and grace;

But the soul that looks through loving eyes,
　Can ne'er know change or decay;
But will still live on, though the substance fades,
And will love you forever and aye.

"AT EVENTIDE IT WILL BE LIGHT."

TO N. B. F.

FOND Mother, while your tearful eye
　In mute appeal, doth gaze
Within my own with longings vain
As you recall the days,

The happy days, now past and gone,
　When dimpled arms were thrown
Around your neck in fond embrace
　While sweet lips pressed your own—

Sweet childish lips, whose every tone
  Was like rich music sweet,
Whose merry laughter echoes now,
  With tread of little feet.

About the quiet haunts of home,
  Within the silent room,
Where you so lonely sit and grieve
  For him, your cherished one,

Torn from your loving heart's embrace
  Ere scarce you'd learned to prize
The Angel to your household sent,
  Child-Angel, in disguise,

Bless God the while! although with tears
  You weep your darling dead,
Though the sweet summer time of hope
  From out your soul has fled,

And Winter winds seem wailing still
  Around the dear ones tomb;
And the sunny sky of faith and trust
  Is shadowed o'er with gloom.

May not your fondest wish and prayer,
  For him your darling boy,
A blest reality become,
  A fount of peace and joy,

When ended is your earthly life?
 And he maturer grown,
Expanded 'neath the heavenly powers
 Shall bid you, "Welcome home!"

Then while there still is left to you
 Another treasure rare,
A bud of promise to unfold
 Beneath your love and care,

Grieve not! but patient wait his time
 And trust that all is right;
Though dark the way, at eventide
 It surely will be light!

GROWING OLD.

O WHY does the thought of growing old
 Cast on us its withering blight?
And why is youth called a radiant morn
And age but a darksome night?

Could we but see the light beyond,
 As we see the setting sun
Tinging the clouds with golden rays
 When the day is almost done,

We should happier be as we neared the verge,
  And our Life's sun sank from view,
For all the clouds of grief and care
  Would be lit with a glorious hue.

And a radiant light from the heavenly dawn
  Would illumine our pathway here,
Making the darksome clouds of age
  Most beautiful and clear,

By which we should see beyond this life—
  Beyond its doubts and fears,
That the life above this cloudy vale
  Is reckoned not by years.

That the loving heart can ne'er grow old,
  Though slowly its pulses beat;
Though the head is silvered o'er with snow
  And the form is feeble and weak.

There is life above, unchanged by time,
  Untouched by earth's decay,
Where Age shall know a glad spring-time
  'Neath the light of an endless day.

A SNOW PICTURE.

ROBED in light O, see them floating!
　　White-winged messengers they seem,
Wafted downward through the ether,
　　Like the spirits of a dream.

Tree and shrub and tender grass blade,
　　Gabled roof and lofty tower,
Share alike the sweet enchantment,
　　Feel the witchery and power,

Of the Artist's skill and cunning:—
　　Who like him can so adorn ?
Change the rudest of earth's pictures
　　Into shapes of grace and form ?

Man may fashion strange devices:
　　Turret, wall and massive dome;
But behold, the wonderous models
　　God has wrought from tree and stone!

Parian wreaths o'erhanging tree tops;
　　Banners white, that, floating fair
From each bough and crested summit,
　　Wave their snowy folds in air.

Who can picture all the beauty?
  Artist's brush can never trace,
Nor the poet's words of fancy
  All the symmetry and grace,

That is here revealed before us;
  Study as we may the plan
Of this wondrous architecture,
  Drawn to please the eye of man.

A NEW YEAR'S REVERIE.

I AM standing on the threshold,
  Looking forward, looking back,
O'er the year that lies behind me,
  To the Future's pathless track!
Shall I venture in the darkness
  On this way as yet untrod,
Leave the Past and all its keeping
  Safely in the hands of God?

Tread this border land—the Future—
  With a firm and fearless tread,
Trusting to a heavenly guidance
  Wheresoe'er I may be led?

Never doubting, never fearing,
  Though the way with thorns be strewn;
Knowing as I onward journey,
  I shall never walk alone ?

Yes, an unseen presence leads me
  Onward o'er Life's trackless way,
And I feel with naught beside me
  It is with me day by day;
That it never, never leaves me
  This unseen but present friend,
Who will guide my wandering footsteps
  Onward to life's journey's end.

And I'll look not back repining
  Where but late I stood in fear
On the threshold, weary, waiting
  For the morning to appear;
For the past is far behind me;
  Angel hands have led the way
Out of sorrow into gladness,
  Out of darkness into day.

OUR MODEL.

WE are the clay, and thou our potter,
    Mold us, Father, to Thy will;
    Shape us by Thine own true pattern,
By Thy wisdom and Thy skill.

Measure us by Thy proportion,
    By Thy fullness and Thy grace;
May no flaw or stain or blemish
    Mar Thy image or deface.

Round our souls to Thy perfection;
    Try us in the furnace heat
Of affliction, if it strengthens,
    Proves us, makes us more complete.

TOO SOON.

TO S. W.

NAY, say not so my agèd friend:
  Though death our fondest hopes may chill,
The fittest time for one to die,
  Is when the Heavenly Father wills.

Too soon for us, but not for them:
  For God hath greater need than we,
And all our times are in his hand;
  His wisdom to the end can see.

And though we mourn the early dead,
  The child of promise, youth of pride,
The fair young maiden in her bloom,
  Know, stricken ones, they have not *died*.

God hath but called them farther on;
  His field of labor stretches wide;
And their brief work that we call done,
  Is but begun the other side.

Too late! alas, too late we learn
   The lesson sent our grief to still;
The lesson Christ the Master taught,
   Submission to God's holy will.

For all things, whatsoe'er of good
   Or seeming ill, the Father sends,
Will work together for our good
   If we but trust Him to the end.

ANNIVERSARY POEM.

"The years have linings, just as goblets do,
The old year is the lining of the new;
Filled with the wine of precious memory
The golden *was* doth line the silver *is*."

THE "Wine of precious memory!"
   O, let us taste the draught,
  From out the silver goblet
  Lined with glimmerings of the past.

Let us gaze into the ruddy depths
   Ere we drink to other years,
And note the changing lights and shades
   The sunshine and the tears.

For to these lives in union blent,
  Mixed with Love's flowing cup,
The bitter and the sweet have been,
  And they have drank it up.

But filled again by God's own hand,
  It daily hath run o'er,
With blessings rich and mercies kind
  Poured from his generous store.

And as to-night we pledge with wine,
  The " Wine of Memory " dear,
How all the gladness of the past
  In its clear depth appears.

How all the joys of wedded life,
  Its loves, its hopes, its fears,
Rise to the surface as we gaze
  Adown the vanished years.

The years since first these loving hearts
  United were in one,
Since merrily rang the marriage bells
  Upon their wedding morn.

But now the noon of life appears
  And resting from its glare
Within this cozy, safe retreat,
  We find the worthy pair,

Still sipping life's rich nectar sweet
　Poured out by love divine—
Let us drink to them from out the cup
　And pledge *long life in wine!*

The "Wine" that cheers, but not allures,
　That strengthens all who taste,
That warms the heart and binds the hand,
　And lights with love the face.

O may their cup of of blessing flow
　As rich, as full, as free,
As it has flowed from out the past,
　This "Wine of Memory."

THE ICE KING.

HO, Ho, Ice King! you have had your reign!
　Your subjects will no longer bow
　In meek submission to your will;
　For Old King Sol, I trow, will loose their chains,
Shake off the bands, that bound then with an iron
　　hold,
　And bid them stand erect once more,
As stout of heart and bold,

As when you fettered limb to limb
And bowed their stately heads with shame,
     And flung their strong arms to the ground
With proud and cold disdain!
     But now, *you're* captive! gone the power
With which you ruled with iron sway!
     Your crown has fallen to the earth;
Its jewels trodden in the way!
     King Sol now sits upon your throne,
The proudest monarch in the land!
     And all your subjects worship him,
For he has rent the bands
     That you with cruel hands did forge;
And 'neath the warmth of his bright ray
     Have bid them lift their heads once more,
And own his gracious sway.

A DREAM.

I DREAMED last night of the loved ones;
 The loved, who from me have fled,
And entered the Gates of the City,
The City of the Dead!

They crossed o'er the mystical river,
 The river that lies between;
They came to my side as in earth-life,
 I can scarcely think I dreamed!

For their forms were so like earth forms,
 There smiles so radiant and bright,
They seemed to dispel the darkness
 And make all around me light.

And they showed to my vision a lily;
 O, fairer than any, I ween
That ever grew in earth-land!
 More beautiful to be seen.

Its petals seemed sparkling with jewels
 That glistened with heavenly dew;
Its form was more graceful in outline,
 And clearer its tint and hue.

And while I gazed with rapture
  On this heavenly blossom pure,
And wondered, half waking, half dreaming,
  What language for me it bore,

From my sight it quickly vanished,
  Borne back to the land of light
To grace the Heavenly Mansions
  Where earth-stain ne'er could blight.

But who shall say I was dreaming?
  That the loved ones ne'er return,
But are with us only in seeming,
  When for them our hearts fondly yearn!

That those spirit-forms beside me
  Came not, as I saw them stand
Bearing that spotless emblem
  That flower from the fadeless land?

Or that a language unwritten,
  Was not wrapped in each delicate fold
Of that heavenly sign and token,
  That spoke to my inmost soul?

That taught me a lesson more lasting
  Than earth-dreams ever impart,
To be like that lily, as stainless,
  As perfect, and pure in heart.

A BIRTHDAY OFFERING.

MY heart goes out in kindly thought
    To you on this birthday,
   But my true pen must speak the words
My lips, forsooth, would say.

But they, I fear, if put to test
    Would play me false, nor dare
To tell the thoughts in uttered tones,
    The thoughts, so like a prayer,

That breathed aloud might lose their power;
    That silence makes complete;
Like the still river in its course,
    Whose water runneth deep.

But there are hidden springs in earth
    Which well up to the ground,
Making the hill-side green and fresh,
    And all things fair around.

So thoughts from out the heart's deep wells
    Oft rise from depths below,
Refreshing those whose thirsty souls
    Feel their sweet overflow.

And though unuttered and unheard,
  Save by the Father's ear,
Yet blessing those on whom bestowed
  With choicest gifts and dear.

So may these thoughts of mine, enrich,
  And fill with fragrance rare,
The path wherein your feet may tread,
  Paved by this earnest prayer,—

That God will keep you safe from harm,
  Within His care alway;
And that His golden light may fall
  On many a bright birthday.

TEACH US TO PRAY.

AT thy mercy seat, O Father,
     When we kneel our vows to pay,
  Teach us what our tongues shall utter;
  Frame the words our lips shall say.

Nor in vain may our petitions,
    Breathed aloud on bended knee,
Rise to Heaven, but find acceptance
    As we lift our souls to thee.

Teach us that the true forgiveness
    That we ask and humbly seek,
In thine ear hath more of meaning
    Than the simple words we speak.

As we freely, without measure,
    Give unto our fellow men,
All our truest love and pity,
    Can we hope for thine again.

When we pray, "O, grant us Father,
    That thy kingdom *here* may come;"
May we not sit idly waiting,
    While the blesséd work's undone!

And when trials fierce o'ertake us,
   If a victory we have won
Over pain and grief and sorrow,
   Then how sweet, "Thy will be done!"

Help us Father! that more truly
   We may live in word and deed,
Like the blessèd Christ and Master!
   Follow where His footsteps lead.

ASLEEP.

WITH the May blossoms so pure and so sweet,
   Dandelions golden, in bloom at her feet.
Dear little Alice has fallen asleep.

Blue-eyed violets, snow-drops so white,
Great yellow buttercups, cheerful and bright,
Why are your blossoms forgotten quite?

Where are the feet that so oft have strayed
Through pastures verdant and flowery glade,
To pluck you, ere you wither and fade?

Have they grown weary along life's way,
Tired of school, of frolic and play,
And stopped to rest this summer day?

Or have they wandered far out of sight,
To fairer fields, and flowers more bright,
Untouched by earthly stain or blight?

O, songster sweet in yon woodland tree,
What is the song you are singing to me?
Hush your warbling so wild and free,

Lest you wake the darling from her sleep!
Keep, keep your fragrance, violets meek,
And hide you in your shady retreat!

Murmur gently, O silver stream,
As you wander through the meadows green,
For Alice lies in a peaceful dream!

With her tired hands folded over her breast,
She lies asleep in a deep, deep rest,
While her spirit wanders amid the blest!

In that land where flowers forever bloom,
Where death can not enter, or sorrow or gloom,
There you will meet your darling soon.

Then lay her to rest with the blossoms white
As pure as her soul, as her heart as light,
While you tearfully murmur "All is right!."

THE FIRST MAY FLOWER.

A TINY bud half buried in the sand,
    Plucked from the hill-side on a winter's day
  And placed within the sunny warmth of home
  Beneath the sunshine with its cheering ray,

When lo! like starlight shining through the gloom,
  A feeble ray at first, then brighter grown,
I watch its petals open to the day
  With childish wonder, I can not disown;

And as I note its fragrance sweet and rare—
  This beauteous springtime blossom that I hold—
Coming to cheer me in the winter time,
  When woods are bare, and winds are chill and cold,

I think of many a sad and lonely life,
  Half buried in the chill and gloom of doubt,
That only needs the cheering warmth of love
  To bring its beauty and its fragrance out.

A pitying hand to pluck it from the mould,
  And place it 'neath the light and love of God,
That thus its feeble petals may expand
  Like this frail flower's, from out the barren sod.

TO MY MOTHER.

WORDS are but feeble to tell, mother,
  The thoughts that come to me
As I sit in the fading twilight,
Musing on home and of thee;
Of all thy goodness and love, mother,
  That made that home so dear;
Of thy kindly welcome greetings;
  Thy parting words of cheer.

Thy patient self-endurance, mother,
  For the children of thy love;
The willing sacrifice thou mad'st,
  'Till called to Heaven above,
Are like blessings dearly prized, mother,
  Now that thy soul has fled,
And the flame upon Love's altar lit,
  Is quenched at last, and dead.

Not dead; but only seeming!
  True love can *never* die;
Thy faithful love, dear mother,
  Lives through eternity,

And will grow bright and brighter
  As the years of our lives go by,
Drawing us nearer and nearer,
  Thy heavenly home on high;

Where we shall meet thee, mother,
  Shall clasp those beautiful hands,
That are beckoning us over the river,
  Into the summer land;
Where our love shall know no parting,
  Our waiting hearts no pain,
But all will be peaceful and happy
  When reunited again.

FARTHER ON.

OFTEN as I dream and wonder
  Like a child, how it will be,
  Comes this thought, above all others,
  Bringing light and joy to me;
Bringing peace, where trouble 'bideth,
  Like the sunshine in a storm,
Through the darkness it comes streaming
  'Twill be better, farther on.

Farther on! But how much farther?
  Shall we forward look with fears;
Count the years or days before us,
  By our blessings or our tears?
O, the mystery of being!
  Living, breathing vital breath!
Who shall say which is the greater
  Earthly life or change called Death?

For this living life of ours,
  That is flittering swiftly by,
Where? we can not help but question
  And to which comes no reply;
Is as deep and strange a mystery
  As the heavenly life can be,
For we *here* can see but dimly,—
  " Face to face " we there shall see.

Face to face! but here we wander,
  Groping through the mists of doubt;
Longing, wondering, fearing, dreaming,
  Of His ways, past finding out;
Faint and heart-sick, worn and weary,
  Still the battle must be won;
Still we struggle, bravely thinking
  'Twill be better farther on.

When our toilsome journey's over,
　And the night of death is passed,
Sweet the thought, a glad to-morrow
　Bright will dawn on us at last.
All the clouds of grief will scatter,
　All our doubts and fears be gone
In the glory of that morning
　That awaits us farther on.

EASTER MORNING.

LO! the dawn of Easter morning!
　　How it gilds the shades of night,
　Throwing o'er the darkened landscape
　Brightest rays of heavenly light;
Scattering far and wide the shadows,
　All earth's dreariness and gloom:
Lifting e'en the shroud of darkness
　From the portals of the tomb.

Angel voices break the stillness
　Of the quiet Sabbath day,
Angel hands unlock the gateway,
　Backward roll the stone away;

Light for darkness! gone the terror
  Of the grave with all its dread!
" Seek no longer sorrowing mourner
  For the living 'midst the dead!"

How that message wakes sweet echoes
  In our hearts each Eastertide,
Wafted to us down the ages,
  "Christ has risen, glorified!"
Life has conquered! death no longer
  O'er us now can hold its sway!
Sing glad voices!   Shout in triumph!
  For the stone is rolled away.

RELEASED.

THE burden is lifted and ended the strife;
    O, Death! thou art welcome, thou bringest
        new life;
For the heart that here hungers, there, there shall
    receive!
The soul that's in trouble shall never more grieve.

The weight of long years press not heavily now;
No change or decay is stamped on the brow;

The long journey over he resteth in peace;
O, Death! thou hast brought him a happy release.

Earth's trials grow dim in the light of that morn;
Its sorrows are lost in the joys that are born;
No doubt nor dread fear, his soul can assail,
For all is made clear behind Death's dark veil.

Light shone in the valley his footsteps to guide;
No weary waiting to reach the bright side;
Though sad the parting O, dear ones, on earth!
Angels rejoice o'er another new birth.

A SONG FOR THE FLAG.

AN INCIDENT IN REAL LIFE.

OFF those distant rock-bound islands,
　　See the vessels held at bay!
And the sailors madly battling,
　　Through the blinding mist and spray,
And the hurricane's fierce tumult,
　　In the face of fearful odds,
With the raging billows round them,
　　And no help save that of God's.

Blindly clinging to the rigging,
  To the broken masts for aid,
Arms outstretched and blanched lips praying
  That the tempest may be stayed;
Hear their cries for help imploring!
  Bruised and bleeding, see them fall!
While the angry sea engulfs them,
  Buries them without a pall.

Through the gathering darkness peering
  Midst those scenes of gloom around,
See that banner wildly streaming!
  List the music of that sound,
High above the wind's wild tumult,
  And the hurricane's fierce breath,
As those brave, heroic seamen,
  Battle in the face of death!

O'er the waves the sound re-echoes;
  On the rising tide it swells;
Chorus of a hundred voices,
  Of a Nation's triumph tells.
Gone is every thought of danger;
  Like true heroes they can die
Bravely at the post of duty,
  While the Old Flag floats on high.

For the music of that anthem
  On the raging tempest borne
Fills their sinking hearts with courage,
  As the wild winds waft it on;
And they sing in accents clearer,
  Though beneath them yawns a grave,
Of their Country's Starry Banner,
  And the free home of the brave.

AT THE LOOM.

SPIRIT garments here we're weaving;
  Garments soiled, or free from stain;
  Growing ever bright and brighter,
  With each victory that we gain.
Every day of patient striving,
  Every trial that we bear,
Serves to make the raiment whiter
  That our souls at last shall wear.

A DREAM OF HOME.

O GOLDEN plumes! in beauty bending
   Beside the wayside as I pass;
What dreams within my soul ye waken!
What memories sweet, but sad alas!

Within my mind are ever stirring
   As I behold your beauty rare;
And thank the good and gracious Giver,
   Who like bestows His love and care,

Upon the wayside blossoms, blooming
   From out the dry and dusty soil,
As on some rare exotic, nurtured
   By aid of human skill and toil.

But with the season of thy coming,
   The pleasant, sunny, Autumn days,
When nature seems to speak His glory
   And give to its creator praise;

When all the earth is wrapped in quiet
   And Sabbath stillness reigns profound,
Ah! then comes back the old, old longing;
   Again I walk the enchanted ground

That leads to that old farm-house yonder,
    That nestled lies, beneath the hill;
Where birch and alder trees grow tender
    Beside the brook, that murmurs still

Along the wayside, green with mosses,
    Where ferns and grasses droop their head,
And goldenrod as though affrighted
    Bows low at sound of human tread.

I call to mind—while thus I wander—
    That still and quiet Autumn day,
When up the old road winding slowly,
    We bore that aged form away.

Away from those home scenes familiar
    On which so oft, he loved to gaze—
The dear old house, the spruce trees yonder,
    And the old maple with its blaze

Of Autumn tints, all red and yellow;
    The goldenrod beside the road
Drooping its golden plumes of beauty
    As though with grief it bore a load.

O, sad yet sunny-eyed October!
    Thou bring'st me joy and grief in one;
Joy for thy rich and golden harvest;
    Grief for the loved who can not come,

To share my joy at thy returning;
  But who I know have gifts more blest;
For they have passed beyond earth's trials
  And found at last Heaven's promised rest.

HE KNOWS.

O THOUGHT, beyond our thought,
  Higher than mortal mind!
Love, deep un-impassioned love,
  Surpassing human kind!
Wisdom, that's greater far
  Than Earth's or earth born kings!
How weak our judgment!
  Foolish, vain, man's idle questionings!

For what are we, beside
  His great infinitude?
Feeble and weak who pray
  To Him for daily food!
Why limit His vast powers
  Whom countless worlds obey!
We, who can scarcely see
  Beyond our little day?

Who walk with blindfold eyes,
  In darkness and in doubt,
Trying in vain to find,
  All of God's meaning out;

Striving to pierce the veil
  That hides Him from our sight.
The veil that we, ourselves have drawn
  Between us and the light.

Better in simple faith
  To trust His guiding hand;
He knows! although the way
  We may not understand!
And through the valleys drear,
  By pathways dark and dim,
He'll safely lead us, if we will
  But trust the end to Him.

THE MEETING AND PARTING OF THE CENTURIES.

ALL the wonders of the nations,
  Their choicest gifts and best,
    Have been laid at thy feet, fair city,
  "Queen City of the West."
All that the present teaches,
  All that the past has taught,
All that the minds of genius,
  With years of toil have wrought;

All the handicraft of woman,
　　All that art and science claims
Have been brought as votive offerings,
　　To the shrine where genius reigns.
And to crown this great achievement
　　Of all ages unsurpassed,
In a fellowship and union,
　　Hands across the seas have clasped,

And have owned a common kinship,
　　Though of different race and creed;
Owned the tie that binds all nations
　　To be one of common need;
That the rights of all are sacred;
　　In each soul some spark divine
That will kindle into brightness,
　　When the rays of knowledge shine.

At this union of the centuries,
　　Where the Past and Present meet;
What the watchword at the portal?
　　Is it victory or defeat?
What the promise of the morrow?
　　Will the golden age soon dawn,
This the herald of its coming,
　　Prayed and waited for so long?

Yes! the rays of right and justice
 Even now illume the sky,
Tokens of that better kingdom,
 That is coming by and by;
When the light of truth and knowledge,
 O'er the whole broad earth shall shine,
And the law of all right living
 Be fulfilled by all mankind.

FLOWERS.

FLOWERS for the bridal, and flowers for the
  burial;
 Beautiful flowers, your mission is twain;
Bringing joy to earth's happy, loved ones,
 Peace to the hearts overburdened with pain.

Lo! how you brighten the chamber of sickness,
 Lifting the shadows and scattering the gloom;
Bringing strength on your dew-laden petals;
 Healing and balm with your wondrous perfume.

Tender the message you bring to the mourner,
 When your bright blossoms like tear-drops are
  shed
Over the graves of earth's fallen heroes;
 Over the young and the beautiful dead.

Dreary were earth without your fresh beauty!
　Lonely the wayside, and barren the spot,
On the brown upland, in forest and meadow,
　Palace of noble, or peasant's rude cot!

Joy of the springtime and glory of summer!
　Why must ye droop 'neath Autumn's rude blast?
Wither and fade in your bloom and your freshness?
　Beauty like thine forever should last!

But not long, O, not long! will ye leave us forsaken;
　Again will your blossoms besprinkle the sod,
Bringing gladness and cheer to hearts that are weary
　Sweet trust in the wisdom and goodness of God!

REGRET.

SAD heart, that maketh constant moan
　　For tearsures gone beyond recall,
　Cease your vain weeping! all are His!
　He giveth and He taketh all.

Without His mercy we are not;
　His life through all our being flows;
His care provideth all our wants;
　His love our every good bestows.

And though some blessings are denied,—
   Blessings that we might overprize,—
He has withheld them for our good;
   For in our weakness, He is wise.

Blinded by fear, we wildly grope,
   And miss the joy the present brings,
Grasping at doubt that holds us fast
   With idle questionings.

O could we tear the veil aside
   That hides us from God's blessèd light,
And let the light of His great love
   Shine on our darkened sight,

We should no longer spend our years
   In vain regrets o'er what has been;
But see 'neath winter's frost and snow,
   Spring's beauteous blossoming.

For what to-day seems dark despair,
   'Neath the warm rays of hope and love,
Oft proves a blessing sent by Him
   To lift us heavenward.

THE UNGUESSED MYSTERY.

THE Future life, " The life to be,"
  Is it still " The unguessed mystery ? "
Do we beat " The soundless doors " in vain
To find our lost ? Will they come again ?

Have you read the " Legend of St. Mark ? "
When " Through the dungeon's vaulted dark,"
His shining robes of light appeared,
The captive youth no longer feared.

For " The cords released their cruel clasp; "
And broken fell the torturer's grasp;
And up " From bondage and the night,"
He passed to freedom and the light.

Shall not our doors of doubt give way
Before the light of reason's ray ?
God's angels! come they not in vain
Like good St. Mark, to break the chain ?

And though our eyes are dull to see,
Or to define the mystery;
Though ear be deaf to catch the flight
Of silver wings through the hush of night,

There are who see the angel tent,
Who hear the heralds God has sent,
And from their holy altars shine
An inner light, that seems divine.

Shall we not in our dark despair
Breathe, as of old, the Prophet's prayer?
"From fear and doubt O, set us free!
Lord, ope our eyes that we may see!"

A MEMORY.

TO M. K. F.

ONLY a sad, sad memory!
 But know, dear friend ere long
  Thy grief to happiness will change;
  Thy sighing into song.

For though 'tis now a memory,
 A blest reality 'twill be,
. When you shall meet the loved and lost
  And once again your darling see.

Be still sad heart! nor longer mourn
 That she has left your dwelling lone!
 The Father willed that you should be
  Just for a litt'e while, alone.

But not alone—God never leaves
   His children comfortless to mourn,
Soon will his messengers of peace
   Descend upon thy heart and home.

And Faith and Love shall bring thee cheer;
   E'en as the dew revives the flower,
Thy drooping soul shall rise refreshed
   Beneath their light and love and power.

Then grieve no more that she has gone
   A little while before thy time;
But let the memory of her love
   Forever round thy pathway shine.

All that was good and true thou hast;
   Nor time nor change can e'er efface
The filial tenderness and love,
   That shone upon thy loved ones face.

Ah! sweet the memory that she leaves!
   As sweet as was the dying song
She sang, the while her spirit bright
   Waited to join the heavenly throng.

Thus did she meet the blissful change!
   Nor feared to hear the angel's call;
To *her*, the messenger called "Death,"
   Must come alike to each and all.

Calmly she yielded to his touch!
  As beautiful in death as life,
She passed unto that heavenly bourne
  Beyond earth's sorrow, care and strife.

O, let her blesséd memory,
  E'en as her presence, light thy home!
Then thou wilt never parted be
  For she will seem no longer gone.

A PRAYER FOR LIGHT.

THOU the Light! as Thou the Giver!
  Ope our eyes that we may see,
The true light that shineth ever,
When our souls look up to Thee!
  Lift the shadows from our being
As the curtains of the night;
  Give our souls a blest awakning,
Bright with rays of heavenly light!

Sun of Righteousness! that shineth
  With a radiance naught can dim;
Shed thy beams of warmth and brightness
  On the darkened soul within!

Light the dawn of each to-morrow,
  With the rays of hope and peace;
Then shall all earth's weary mortals
Find from pain, a glad release!

ALL IN ALL.

HOW can we dwell from Thee apart
  Whose image mirrored in our heart
    Shows us how good and great Thou art!

Whose love hath neither mete nor bound!
Embracing all, in all things found,
Encompassing the wide earth round.

Whose wisdom planned the mighty whole!
Maker of body and of soul!
O'er all things holdest Thou control.

Thou givest life and breath to all!
The high and low, the great and small;
And heedest e'en a sparrow's fall!

Thou keepest our frail lives in thine!
Weak creatures, why should we repine
When we Thy laws can not divine?

Thy thoughts are far above our own!
We are but finite, Thou alone
Art infinite, O, mighty One!

And in Thy great infinitude,
Thou orderest all things for our good,
If but Thy laws were understood!

Grant us Thy wisdom! May we still
Through all life's changes, good or ill,
Trace but the workings of Thy will.

And where we can not understand,
Trust, Father, to Thy guiding hand;
Thy sternest law, but love's command!

www.ingramcontent.com/pod-product-compliance
Lightning Source LLC
Chambersburg PA
CBHW021536270326
41930CB00008B/1277